Watching for the Hawk

Breda Spaight

WATCHING FOR THE HAWK

Watching for the Hawk

is published in 2023 by
ARLEN HOUSE
42 Grange Abbey Road
Baldoyle
Dublin 13
Ireland
Phone: 00 353 86 8360236
arlenhouse@gmail.com
www.arlenhouse.ie

978–1–85132–304–3, *paperback*

Distributed internationally by
SYRACUSE UNIVERSITY PRESS
621 Skytop Road, Suite 110
Syracuse
NY 13244–5290
USA
Phone: 315–443–5534
supress@syr.edu
syracuseuniversitypress.syr.edu

Typesetting by Arlen House

cover image
by Steve Johnson
is reproduced courtesy of the artist

Contents

ACKNOWLEDGEMENTS

Grateful acknowledgement goes to the editors of the following journals and anthologies in which these poems, often in earlier versions, first appeared:

Abridged: 'My First Sky'
Ambit: 'Soothsayer'
Atticus Review: 'Night Walk with My Mother'
Banshee: 'Safe Period', 'Windfalls'
Best British and Irish Poets (Eyewear, 2018): 'My Mother's Will'
Communion Arts Journal: 'Bacon'
Crannóg: 'Bog'
Cyphers: 'Her Last'
The Honest Ulsterman: 'What My Father Was'
The Interpreter's House: 'My Parents' First Night, 1955', 'The Journey Back'
The Lonely Crowd: 'Final Visit to Her Homeplace', 'Life Lesson', 'On Her Return from Hospital'
The North: 'Music Lesson'
The Ofi Press: 'Tally Stick'
The Ogham Stone: 'Mother Love'
Orbis: 'That Man'
The SHOp: 'Back Kitchen', 'A Fly Death-flays'
Skylight 47: 'My Grandmother's Kitchen: Sketch at 4', 'Final Cut', 'Ash'
The Stinging Fly: 'On the Run in Dreary Eden', 'Solitaire', 'The Night Feed'
Washing Windows III: 'Fish'

For their immense contributions, insights, and generosity of spirit, thanks to the Thursday afternoon poetry workshop in the Galway Arts Centre, facilitated by the late Kevin Higgins, where many of these poems first aired. Thank you all!

I own my deepest gratitude to Jo Slade who curated this collection. Jo, as mentor, also created a space for me to experiment and stretch. Thanks to Words Ireland National Mentoring Programme for the opportunity.

Thank you, Alan Hayes at Arlen House.

I acknowledge the Irish Arts Council's bursary award towards the completion of this collection, and also the Munster Literature Centre for their Covid-19 Literature Bursary.

A family is a mystery.
Sharon Olds

WATCHING FOR THE HAWK

Legacy

She leaves a threadbare coat
laid out like a crucifix.

I feel the shape of her arms
in the cold lining of the sleeves,

slip into them as though into a vein,
forever nailed to her bones.

On the Run in Dreary Eden

Seán Ó Faoláin coined the phrase
'de Valera's dreary Eden'

Even without the gun
and without the car, my parents, a Free State couple,
in their wedding photo, scarcely smiling
on church steps, look like Bonnie & Clyde.
Their thoughts on the run towards each other's
virgin body: for him, skin to skin. Her beefy breasts
he already knows through her blouse. For her:
joined below the belly. The times he cupped her hand,
coaxed her to hold it, he guiding the stroke until
his body's clench spat spit like bird shit
– neither his sin nor hers. Her struggle
to keep his hands from there, there.
She throbbed and prayed, and prayed
when his finger's flick opened her. Her
soul stained.

I grapple with their language, *marriage act,* when I think
of their young bodies pulsing; their seduction swamped
by the catechism of shame; their sounds muffled
even from their own ears – whispery breath of collusion.

They are old Ireland:
born to live the sub-life of delinquents.

They never celebrated their anniversary. I grieve
for never choosing a card to honour the union
that gave me life. I grieve for his wide-leg trousers
and striped tie; her feet dainty in black court shoes.
I grieve for the last four of eighteen siblings farmed out to
neighbours; the three who died that I never knew.

My parents glare from the black-and-white past,
the planes of Oklahoma spread before them,
a vein of blacktop petering into a golden sunset.

My Parents' First Night, 1955

My soon-to-be mother lies awake
under my soon-to-be father,
one body the shadow of the other;
his like the crucified remains of Jesus
fallen from the cross directly on her,
his arms outstretched as though still nailed.
The imprint of his flesh, its ridges and furrows,
pubic hair curled like fossils are stamped in her blood
– a seal, a red disc that cools between them.
Her upturned palms are on the pillow,
a horror film pose of terror or surrender.
Her between-the-legs-place is numb as she wonders
if much of what he did was a sin. The dead weight
of him as he sleeps; limp shoulders
against her breastbone.
She eyes his trousers on the chair back; necktie looped
on the bedpost; the laces of his brown shoes still done.
The first throb in her eardrums earlier when
her hands trailed down the tapered camber of his waist
to the marvel of his backside, cool flesh balloon-soft.
The air around them simmered with animal odour;
their skin popping apart in licks of sweat as they slid
over each other – and then. Then. How he rocked
and rocked as though he'd forgotten her
name, her body hammered like punishment
until he fell from her: a birth – her body
alone in the mountain of dark that sobs
into daylight's last hour.

ZYGOTE

In my half-world as ovum, pearl of my mother,
the time has come for me to fly the nest, sure
and scared as a fledgling; to hover
momentarily between heaven and nothing,
to sense the updraft from the fimbria, to swim
towards those beckoning fingers, pretty as petals,
precious funnel of the fallopian tube, and to glide
there like the bride my mother is, coming
now towards the man who will be my father.
He enters, nudges the hymen, the curtain
of tissue broken. O to hear it tear, a burp; joy
like the joy of first light – the snow cloud of cum
in which I bathe, through which I whirl, choosey
as my mother at a dance; the tall stranger
who tangos like no other, who kisses her
hot as life, hot as the thrust to my shell.
I've sensed her dream of the swaddled prize
from her womb: hair black as *hers, her* brown eyes,
her known world. My yolk pierced now,
bright light collision of two worlds,
each particle blasted, consummated, fused
to the chasm in my mother's dream: the helix
of a red-haired, blue-eyed man, the sulk in him – the light
i float towards and die; resurrected as zygote;
divide, multiply; two, four, eight: the carve up begins.

Reaping Place

My birth canal memory is that she is small,
smothering, when I writhe from her womb
– our womb – our time of longing
for each other's face. The loneliness
ruptured by the crush of a contraction
– my first hurt by her; vibrations that arc
from her tailbone to mine as her screams
spiral up my backbone, stalling me,
like that day a decade on
when she says, *You're just like*
your father. Useless!
I don't know where to turn,
my right shoulder wedged
against her pelvic bone,
my body ambushed by her
body, as though she can't let go.
My crowned head hangs like a turtle's,
the flesh of her vulva around my neck firm
as a kiss-locked mouth; her heartbeat
a thrum now from another room, the sound
at first either mine or hers; while my wrinkled feet,
with all the wisdom of an elephant's,
take a last touch of our reaping place.

If

If she'd called the Gardaí, they'd see
my mother and me eyeball each other in the kitchen.
If she'd called the Gardaí, they'd recognise the smell of
blood, her blood; the tang of my first milks – sugars
sucked from her breasts, iron from her umbilical.
If she'd called the Gardaí, they'd notice
the razorblade held aloft by my mother
like a priest honours the raised host.
If she'd called the Gardaí, the female Garda
would view my mother as caught red-handed.
If she'd called the Gardaí, they'd observe
blood on the razorblade, track its teardrop
trickle down the blade's edge, down
her index fingernail's shiny, pink surface,
a crescent of red under her thumbnail. See it
ripple over her knuckle wrinkles.
If she'd called the Gardaí,
the male Garda would say, *What happened here?* Black
notebook in one hand, black pen poised in the other.
If she'd called the Gardaí, she'd repeat what she'd said
when she found the blade, *Who put this in my shoe?*
The razorblade would quiver.
The geraniums would quiver.
The words would quiver
from the black ink onto the white page.
Fingerprints would be dusted for in that house
where touch was threat. Cameras would haul
light into the loveless corners. The bloody
blade would be bagged, tagged. Evidence.
A high-vis medic would bandage my mother's big toe.
If she'd called the Gardaí, the female Garda
would reassure me, *Your Mam will be ok.*
The blade would lay boxed on a metal shelf
in a room of shelves of similar boxes.

The case would become a cold case, a case
the authorities forget, until one night, let's say,
a frosty night in January 40 years later, someone
phones the Garda confidential line. For argument sake,
let's say it's a woman. Let's say she's been smoking
in the backyard at 2am. Stars cut the dark
with stamps of story long dead. She hesitates
on the line. Her voice breaks, *If she'd*
loved me, she says. *If she'd only loved me.*

Safe Period

After her third child, X marks the forbidden
days, and my mother sleeps in my bed, sour
in her heat – summer Sunday seaside odour.
Odd nights when she's suddenly beside me;
my back to the wall, proper as a doll; rosaries
chanting through her damp fingers until cockcrow;
prayer and seed coursing to her womb, the Our Father,
Hail Mary mumbled to the inner chant
– I hope I've escaped,
this time.
Days when the house is a chorus to
her strain; doors bang, pots clatter:
she loathes her nature,
not sex, but holding him, his whispered doubts
pleasure to her heart, a fault
before Christ the redeemer, the child
a curse, mishaps buried like pups in dung heaps.
They avoid each other
in the evenings, the *Please* and *Thank you*
of strangers; air crackling with unspent sex
worrying every cell, bodies hunched over
chairs, kneeling for the Rosary. Even I notice
the curve of her backside through the arc of his gaze;
his voice leading hers; all of us clustered,
as though the last people on a wreck.

What My Father Was

I see him now so clearly
as he plays the melodeon – the box
he calls it – firm as a limb on his left knee,
dandelion pleats corrugating dusk onto his narrow face.
Like a goat, the bass side butts as he draws and shoves.
His body is a prize fighter's when viewed from behind,
lanky shoulders and elbows punched-poised, shadow
boxing in the radio's gold robe of light as a new tune
wrestles him. The notes inseminate his body – the throe
of a hip, lurch of his backbone; ribs listening
as he consummates the melody that ploughs
towards his joyous self,
that morsel of him
                    that dies daily
                                        and rises at twilight
– the resurrected pure being of my father.
If I saw only his slender neck in an open collar
white Sunday shirt, I'd know all about his bachelorhood
playing music at the crossroad; offerings of bottled stout
like ten pins around his feet; flurry of red whirling skirts;
echoes of *Sound man yourself!* He anticipates the applause
like thirst awaits rain.
In a '50s cloth cap, I become
the young man forged cruel by his gift, lapping up praise,
yet aware of how effortless music is for him
– The fools, the óinseachs,
                              or is he the dolt?
the crowd humouring him as nightfall's slow
descent describes the day, enclosing everyone
in the ordinary virtues that unchain them.

MUSIC LESSON

First to saddle my lap is a doll, last
is my parents' last child. In between
is my mother's notion that I should sit
beside that man, my father, and learn
to play his melodeon. It is all wrong,
like knowing I should not
touch a nettle,
and do, and get stung,
and watch the red hive
plump; the sob from my mouth –
lips not yet muscled by language.
This time, he takes my hand. This time, he spreads
my fingers. This time, to touch the cool white buttons
and it is the same old tune –
pull, push, slow, slower, gently, faster.
Afterwards, the silence. He is gone. I
stand cool and hard in the absence
of his stop/start breath, mid-chest pant,
his tobacco-stained false teeth. For now, the pain
is normal. You know: the one where you lose
sight of your parents on a crowded beach,
that pounding heart fright of
which way is home?

Lemass

When I hear that name, I see
again the hole in the wall where my father
hammers a nail to hang new curtains. The flexors
of his freckled arm narrow to his wrist, the nail
held between finger and thumb.
I now see that his hunched shoulders
are a farm labourer's inheritance. His fingers
are also warped, muscle-bound, as though
forged to only milk a cow. He continues
to pound the nail – wet pebble smell
of cement, his smell
now that he is a builders' labourer.

He says, *What're y' looking at, useless?*
I've learned to outstare him – not bravery,
but fear gone full circle. He seems boxed-in,
as though he'd rather be planting cabbage
or playing rebel airs on the melodeon.
At times, a fragment of joy hovers
just beyond him, a feeling opposite to love
or hate: the hope of finding myself in a story
without him. He holds a nail in his mouth, a horse
with the bit between its teeth.
I see the shallow hole – gouged concrete
like a jagged splash of hollowed out grey.
Scattered plaster speckles the red lino.
The nail is bent double.

That Man

Mental asylum: my first big words –
motherese for sad man and my mother drinking
tea at the front wall on summer Tuesdays.

Her voice cords with his. Words sung
in each other's face; spun-out film noir
mumbles; something late night, Ingrid Bergman.
Sudden silence like the abrupt black

of a blank television screen on a couple
kissing; frisson between her and my father
amid the kitchen smell of second day stew
and squandered flesh.

On those heat hazed afternoons, chestnut horses
in Madden's furlong field tongue each other's
withers, neck, flank;

tail-swish, swish;
wind among pampas; swish
across steppe:

two mugs in the sink,
teardrop tea stains.

The Washing Machine Demo Man & My Mother

after Natalie Diaz

You and the man
stand beside the white round washing machine,
a couple toppled from a wedding cake.

In the kitchen, without an apron, you
are slick as a stalking cat.

This morning, best sheets engulf many other wives
and their demo man. A wife in Offaly

loads her washer, mounds of Churching
folded in her sheets, like you'd fold a letter to the devil.

A wife in Sligo packs her drum with as much
rhythm method she can stamp on her sheets,
like flowers stamped on the devil's face.
The demo man cautions against overloading.
She says, *Fuck off.*

In Ballybog, a wife feeds her wedding dress
into boiling suds foamy as perpetual virginity.

Somewhere someone takes the hand
of their demo man, closes his fingers over her breast.

The machine throbs like the heart of a stalking cat.

Pity my mother. All exposed waist and curvy curves
as she endeavours to coax these four walls
into the washer, the Sacred Heart picture
on the floor by the door like a rodent she'd rout.

If there's an Archangel
of the washing machine demo man,
and he's the one to restore her knowledge,
then, Dear Archangel, appear to her
tomorrow.

Her Cross

When I drink, it is always 1967.
The dog lies still on the frozen grass, white blades
bowed under blinking crystals. The chain from its neck
to the conifer is muddied and knotted like a root
from which it draws life. I remember it as a pup,
like all the pups my father ever brought home
when drunk; the milky smell of its vigorous body,
fonts of sorrow in sloe-black irises.
What do we have here? What is this?

He produces the pup from his coat pocket carefully
as a birth, his face at its most wounded:
he could cry, vomit or even laugh, the pup
held high like a boyhood memory beyond reach
yet as close as yesterday, alcohol collapsing time
like time in a fairytale.

The pup ends up tied to a tree, savage;
the half-moon it inhabits no larger than ours,
grass worn down like chewed fingernails,
the verge jagged as the amber outline of piss stains
on the bedwetter's sheets.

To give my father his due, he never slaughters a dog
that hasn't first bitten him. He stands with a pitchfork
at the edge of Rex-Prince-Spot's sphere of mud, goading
– a flagellant coveting his own blood,
scourging his sin, craving a cure
stronger than drink to kill
another tomorrow;
my mother's mouth red as a cut,
Christ, not in front of ...

What's in a Word

When my father says, *She'll soon get enough of it,*
the words swirling from his mouth, skating
over the thin ice of the kitchen, I look at you,
your face furrowed by the black-and-white
flicker of the television, where a man and woman kiss,
you buttoned up in a cardigan, tied in by an apron
the way a secret is tied down in the body, and
suddenly I sense your anger. I don't understand
what my father has said, all I know is that
suddenly the kitchen freezes. Your hair
looks frost slumped, your face white
as sleet-dusted stone, your gaze
like that of someone about to glaciate.
For so long I have wanted you
to grasp joy by the hand and swim
through our lives. Now I sense that joy
requires a medium, like how time stopped
when the woman's lips met the man's lips.
You say, *She doesn't love him.*
Your vowels clink in the room
like splintering crystal. A gleam of triumph
wavers at the corners of your eyes. It's as though
you've dared to rob from my father. A cloudburst
of words hail from his mouth, a rumble
around one new word, he pronouncing
the word slowly, perhaps unused to saying the word
– *somethingsomethingsomething the foreskin saga.*
His upper teeth sank
into his lower lip as if to steady the *f*
on the tongue, like a surgeon steadies the knife
that envisions the wound. The droop of your mouth
says that the word slapped you. Awakened, you
are now in an arctic region, an unexplored place
that I've come to value as your woman rage. Opposite

feelings crowd your face, a captive's fine facial gestures – lowly/exalted, impassive/hopeful. You communicate with me – caution me, alert me to examine what I see, but I don't know what I see. My father's mouth shut firm, as though he's said it all, and if he hears another word, is ready to say more.

The Homeplace

She is going home:
no longer truly ours.
Even the light steals her;

skin a shade lighter, intensifying the black of her hair;
eyes alive in a scene of nibbling sheep.

She times the journey to miss mass
in Ennis, Crusheen and Gort. The Morris Minor
glimmers through narrow streets as each town funnels
into a landscape where hedgerows yield to drystone walls
– stippled rock reaped from thin-grassed fields.

She turns to us, huge in her absence, as though we are
supine and she's falling, falling. She licks her fingers
to smoothen our hair, our smiles.

Ahead now is her homeplace.
The crooked row of *cypress leylandii* forms a windbreak
to the south-west of the house. Turf rick part igloo home
for dogs; the yard a muddle of hens, geese; cautious cats
sat like camels on windowsills. My mother's mid-stride
feet in a nanosecond of flight on her run to the back door.

Within, a puppet show.
Her troupe takes her coat, kisses her; while we wonder
at the pewter patina of windows. Split coal black
roof slates; pup belly pink quoin stones;

light's precise splendour keeping our mother close,
as though it's our duty to bind ourselves
to the place she loves.

My Grandmother's Kitchen:
Sketch at 4

Dressed in layers of black skirts
and cardigans, my grandmother
fusses around the giant hole
of the open hearth, a conductor
conducting an orchestra of pots.
She's on the threshold of witchhood
as she stirs and pokes a cauldron of stew.
Her herding arms say, *I love you,*
let me feed you; foster a feeling of being
in myself as I roam among yellow chairs
embossed with bluebells, delft decorated
with pheasant or otter. I seek a hidden door.
And when I see the open red purse
of my mother's mouth, the creased oblongs
of her eyes, chocolate irises bracketed
by slivers of white, I feel as though
I'm on a magic carpet about to crash
– she is smiling. I remember the wonder,
like coming to a stop after spinning around
and around: my first time to sense
I'd never truly know her.

Tally Stick

i.m. my maternal grandparents

When I learn about the tally stick
hung from your schoolchild necks with twine, I am
tongue-tied, concentration-camp-gaunt. African slave.
Choctaw. Aborigine. Whale:

and you are Murphy's dog, Bran; block of timber hung
from his collar impeding the chase – cars, women joggers,
fat tongues on their trainers.

The pendulum of wood skins Bran's neck raw-pink,
deep-pink of baby tongue. His legs fare worse as flesh
peels to bone: femur notched for misdemeanours.

Unable to curl for sleep, Bran loses the dream
of running, sheds it from muscle stretched readily as lung;
piston limbs; hound of hounds on gorse hillsides;
Fionn mac Cumhaill tales of mighty pursuits
flowing off his tongue.

I, daughter of your daughter,
hear you chatter by the hearth – unknowable
words in a guttural idiom. How you say *fhy* instead of *why*;
shimmering bubbles bursting on tongues.

The Back Kitchen

It has the chill of a cave.
Galvanised buckets of cream
never curdle here; its almond odour
seeps through muslin cloths – squat brides
on the table beneath the crucifix
next to the hook from which the Sunday goose hangs
by corn yellow legs; its tube of neck wrapped
in newspaper, bound with twine, leaking drip drips
of blood into the enamel basin; spatter patterns detonating
on its white sides. A room of shelves and silhouettes;
brown packages of tea leaves, sugar,
a four-stone bag of flour on a stool like a plump child;
the wooden butter churns like pirates' casks
under the Belfast sink.

My grandmother waits for my mother here
– the married daughter,
the motorcar, new house in another place
she can only picture. In her visitor clothes
my mother's arms are outstretched with oriental poise
as my grandmother dresses her in a wraparound apron,
circles her – knowing she longs for this:
butter churns in the centre of the room,
leisurely flow of cream – no splash, thick liquid
supping itself. Finally, the lid set in place; knock
of wood against wood ancient as trees.
She turns the handle, laughs, laughs.

Outside, day spins towards dusk, lengthens my father's
sundial shadow as he leans against the wing of the car.

The Journey Back

My father honks the horn. My mother's time is up.
Her people orbit the Morris Minor; stock the boot
with bags of turf, potatoes. Aunt Monica in her apron
showers holy water on the windscreen, crosses herself,
then nuzzles me through the open window. I know
such love only with her.

She and my mother as girls plucked berries here,
trampled brambles, spread their legs on the plough horse.
Shared the blood code respect for scarce food – pigs
fed, chickens minded from the hawk. Dogs at their heels,
they picked May altar cowslips, the sky bleached
by nearby ocean reflecting radiance off limestone fields.

From the back door to the car is my mother's path now.
Her Jackie Kennedy coat and dress outfit is graceless
at the wrist, wrists bred from forefathers who milked
at dawn and dusk. My mother and Aunt Monica nudge
cheeks like cats. It hurts to see them hug, their shape
lonesome – a standing stone: foreheads to different winds.

BOG

*

Fairies blue flames flicker at dusk.
Come nightfall, the flight of snipe toss stars
to the heavens. I don't believe my eyes,
or my mother.

*

Bog hole bad dream – swallowed thoroughly as an oak,
envoy from an age when trees were holy. My mother
forever wary of the journey.

*

We watch the collies puff sheep
through a stone gap on the mountain field.
Its name ingrained for generations.

I want to say, *It's only a hill,*
but my palm is warm in hers, and her language
of landscape, words from hand-me-down memory,
can never be mine.

*

Head and shoulders, black-clothed people walk
among drystone walls stark as crows
in this treeless place – specks in distant fields
either man or beast mistaken for rock.

Her face is her soul here; lips pursed, eyes
seeing beyond us – the sight of herself as dust.

Home

Oak

When my father left
for work in the cement factory,
my mother would flap
her apron and lob it
on the back of a chair,
joggle from slippers
into black Wellingtons, gird
her head in a scarf knotted
under her chin, hunch
into an old overcoat of his
and go milk the cow; the one
task that wooed her back
to her fields flecked with stone, far
from these pastures overhung with oak.
Words like mastitis and brucellosis
sang through my childhood, until
the day the teacher said, *You'd think*
you'd a farm.

Ash

The locals ravage the storm-felled ash in hours.
Men scuttle for all points to the Major's field,
a Charlie Chaplin montage of toing and froing; tractors,
drays, chainsaws and crosscuts. My father is among them,
a stranger to my mother as she turns from the window.
She holds his shirt, inhales what she is sure of.

His heart warped by history is new to her,
a Golden Vale cottage boy on the four mile walk to school
hemmed in by the high, mortared wall:
TRESPASSERS WILL BE PROSECUTED
the red letters on white metal signs nailed to tree trunks:
bullet-pocked on New Year's Eve.

Shouldered by the brothers-in-law, the bough of ash
is trophy-like. She hears my father laugh. Her clenched
fingers scrunch his shirt. The men's backroom tones
continuing into the night.

Whitethorn

Her best muslin dress strains over her first.
Dishcloths are drying on the whitethorn hedge.
The sun breaches cloud. She does not know

that the boy will resemble her, that she'll snag her dress
many's the day before truly knowing a hedge. Drifts
of white blooms in May, the ruby berries of autumn; naked
as the winter night she'll nurse her newborn.

His pupils will reflect her face: his eyes a sanctuary,
a hedge to sculpt. She'll learn to slash sturdy limbs,
crimp pliant saplings.

My Grandmother's Kitchen:
Sketch at 8

Wooden as a string puppet, my grandfather
lies in the white ruffles and lace of the coffin.
My mother touches his face as though she decodes
the parchment-like skin of his unselfing. A croak
like the original tremor of language rises
from the women dressed in black who beetle
through the room. Other voices merge,
an almost sweet sound like a hive's hum; a storm
brewing – only to falter
as each woman surrenders
and keens from her own sorrow.
I'm high on lemonade. Candlelit shadows
mount the walls, blot part of us into the dark.
I'm afraid and want to go home. My mother
is unlike my mother: she is like a fish in a shoal,
the pressure sense of their bodies creating a contour
that twists and turns; their world sealed. Face after face
could be hers: my first time to sense
she belongs only there.

Spawn

My mother says herr*ings* now as opposed to *herrin.*
It's something to do with my school shirt and tie.

I'm 12, immersed in language as a fish
is unaware of water; afloat on the word *first*:
first blot of blood cast like spawn splash of trout; in first
year in secondary school; first to do so in my family tree.

Alone for the first time in my mother's kitchen,
the room wrestling with dawn, currents of questions
eddy around her black rosaries hung from
the Sacred Heart lamp.

She bought everything on the school booklist,
including the *Bible.*

When I look in on her for the first time, I know her
bedroom is a room without dreams; tattered
coral rose wallpaper blisters over conduit
funnelling power

to the bedside lamp; the amaranth-edged pages of
her prayer book the colour of lipstick
popular among the big girls.

I catch sight of myself in her mirror. Those ringlets
she makes me wear, and those brown Mary-Janes.

I practice my new smile, moisten my lips
with my tongue first.

Watching for the Hawk

I love him. I hate him.
He hovers over the chicken run,
his brown body tacked to the sky, buff
underbelly streaked blackish suddenly
hanging there, peaceful as the holy dove.
That fine bird enthrals me, and those yellow
fluffy chicks wobbly on their yellow legs
– yet something lethal in the air.
I think of my mother, flour raining through her fingers;
pinch of bread soda ground first between her palms,
our daily bread seasoned by her body's salt. She prays
to a priest's back on Sunday, while on the radio
politicians discuss their economic plan. I leave her
at the table, lifelines of her palms obliterated
again and again from the dough she kneads.
I view the scene as though watching for the hawk:
my heart throbbing, the scream in my throat.

A Fly Death Flays

on the amber spiral of flypaper,
its hiss in tune with my mother's listless feet

as she paces the bright, tiled kitchen, shaking
the two pint brown bottle in both hands
in which she makes butter.

I swam inside her once, before which I lay in wait,
no face, she hymen-locked: our purest time.

Everything between us was a dream. I as much of her
parents and theirs; she not yet hurt, or hurtful;
a daughter churning cream in wooden butter churns,

her body's rhythm in rhythm with her mother's,
and grandmother's and hers; melody that instilled
ovum-me with an awareness of when music stops.

She pokes butter blobs through the bottleneck
with a knitting needle; scent of almond, dawn, wild garlic;
her eyes close corpse solid, *Just for the taste.*

The fly, wings outstretched; iridescent
in an angle of evening light,
tranquil; poised as though for flight.

Blood

Those buckets of blood
bothered me once I knew
it was my mother's. Before
knowing, I believed it was
pig's.

The day she and my father heaved
the howling sow onto a board
propped on blocks. Madden
with his knife, blessed himself,
slashed its neck.

How can she be a mother?
She brushes the range top
with a goose wing;
cuddles brown hens
then axes their heads.
Her underwear bleeds in water.

Fish

She runs the blade
through the gill's silvery flap,
hews the head twice, three times, four;
severs bone, the knife's handle solid
in the oblique arch of her right hand,
her left a wolf's paw holding down fresh catch,
its slipper-like body, mouth open as death
sang its last note of ocean breath. She makes the first cut
to the white belly, a wound like Christ's on the cross,
from where she drags plum, slithering, knotted
entrails; her face childlike; eyes, mouth set as though
freed by the rhythm of ritual, governed by knowledge
leached from her marrow as she steers out the pearly
treasure of the ovaries, roe glistening in her palm.
I am there, a library book on my lap. Each page turned
affirms the story of this woman, my mother, standing
over severed heads with furious eyes; her fingers laced
with luminous scales – for now, a she-warrior,
queen of her domain.

BACON

I still see her fold in half, one leg ballerina-
raised for balance as she bows into the wooden
barrel for next day's flitch of bacon.

My brother wears his cowboy suit; black hat,
leatherette waistcoat with fringes across the chest.
His gun holster buckle is the Lone Star.

Meat steeps in a bowl of water overnight.
Salt liquefies; spume rises and floats while
she sleeps in a house of thunder; moths furred

bodies pattering the whore-red glow of
the Sacred Heart lamp on the kitchen window.
The Virginian's gun is under his pillow.

She slices bacon with her loneliness, the air
marbled various auras of sad: dawn, midnight,
August. The long years of her love like

starlight's colossal dying. John Wayne
at the kitchen door, *I'm the sheriff 'round here.*
Hands in the air, an' nobody gets hurt.

Night Walk with My Mother

She says, *Don't ever get married.*
If only I had my life to live all over.
We see golden lamp-lit sitting rooms.
She says, *Isn't the moon lovely.*
I never knew it could be so bright.
We hear cats yowl ghostly in farmyards.
She says, *I need air.*
She mops her eyes with a hanky.
She says, *A man's heart is his own.*
It's the way they are. Spoiled by mothers.
Narrow weasels and humped rats cross our path.
She says all sorts of things.
She blows her nose.
We bless ourselves passing the graveyard.
If I hadn't had kids.
If I could only drive.
If there were more chances for us.
She says. *I need air.*
She says, *Don't ever get married.*
You'll know soon enough.
We see trees lace patterns tremble on the road.
Don't say I didn't try to warn you.
Mind your education.
Stay away from them.
Keep yourself pure.
She says all sorts of things.

THE SUMMER OF LOVE

Today I think about that crocheted poncho
my mother made for me – turquoise
flecked with orange. It had tassels.
I'd never seen one; a time
when dormant hormones lurked
in my routine of school and home.
The outside world was a herd
of something new and wanton
only my mother saw – young people
dressed in psychedelic clothes,
bearded boys with hair like Jesus.
She popped the poncho on herself
to demonstrate its style. Arms spread,
a dervish, she whirled and spun
– one of her good days; the past
a corpse, the future in hide-and-seek mode.
Or was the animal in her restored after
the plain and purl of cardigans and jumpers?
Even her pots and pans deemed her remote.
She looked as though she could saunter
to another house where she was the daughter.

O my! Did she want us to hold hands
and run like sisters into the blue ocean,
to flit like butterflies, to sup nectar from lilacs,
to be born into the gold, gold days of that summer?

The Suitcase

By now, I'm a collector of secrets.
I seek mute corners, sift dream from the half-remembered,
meaning from the half-known – staccato night whispers
in the kitchen; the long silence. Bone-white elbow tip,
all that's seen of my father's arm under my mother's skirt
in the orchard that sunny day, her toes clenching grass,
the shudder in her voice, nettle sting shock
ripping between my legs. I move silently
against the scent of their bedroom,
against white light soaked from sheets stretched skin tight,
the black suitcase beneath the bed; the lining, blood-red as
blood, dotted with dot-size, white stars, carnival in scale,
my mother's old dresses – blues, greens, pinks, black and
white stripes, vital shades in a magician's trick.
I covet them,
as though knowing the burn of a man's hand
on a body that looms in me, one I recognise in slim, belted
shapes I drag from her raw self, a girl who flirted, jived,
her dress flared like the bloom of a foxglove, her core
signalling its want for me in her womb, not knowing
that in giving me life I will seize everything from her.

SOLITAIRE

My mother played cards all summer.
Hunched for hours at the table, light from the window
at her back, the lob-sided layout of solitaire enclosed
by her arms.

Was it the year her father died?
Columns of order, queen under king, jack under queen,
her way of numbing her heart. Or was it the year
she finally let go of the cow?

This woman who sat only in the evening, her lap
busy with sewing or knitting; the pink flesh of her fingers
a sheath for worked muscles. She radiated peace, at home
in her body's tempo – a rhythm that shaped the air.

I lived close to her sadness. I sat in the same room
and never heard her altered breath. Card sliced
against card as she shuffled the deck.

Final Cut

The clash of shovel against stone
carries from the haggard to the kitchen
where my mother and I watch television. Alone
we take the men's chairs beside the cream and black range.

Alone, we are women; she forty-five, seven months
gone and I menstruating; a Leaving Cert student; first
of my kind from bog-ignorant Ireland.

The Mary Tyler Moore Show is on; with her career,
apartment and apparently no man, she is sheer porn-
ography, arousing rebellion and regret between us:
the fault line that of last comely maiden,
and first material girl.

I've not slit a hen's neck, legs flecked with hot blood;
a rite eclipsed when I stepped onto the free school bus;
indifferent to my mother's world, bar the memory of
her knife hand pulling the faithful cut:
a violinist drawing the final note.

Her Last

My mother, forty-five – another child,
opens the door to Nurse Begley, all smiles
and too much pine air freshener. I had forgotten
how beautiful her face is, rinsed with innocence,
as though under a spell. And her hair like a moonlit lake
– black with silver ripples. I notice when her voice
becomes high pitched, like she's about to sing
or scream; talking about her bowels
as though she shares the secret of her days
when she does not get up, nights she ignores
the baby's cry. Whatever life she had is over:
soda bread cooling on the window, nappies boiling
in the pot. The story she tells of my birth in this house,
how Mrs Hayes from over the road was there to help.
She talks and talks, stares long into Nurse Begley's face,
her eyes wide as a swimmer's who realises
they're out too far. I worry she'll choke mid-word,
will clutch Nurse Begley and pull her down, curl into her
like a child, in the cooling rays of the sun.

THE NIGHT FEED

Blankets lift, cold air stuns
my skin as my mother huddles
the new baby from the cot.
She waggles the tartan-blue flask
before pouring the formula, slow milky flow
puffing a dawn breath of vapour. She holds
the bottle to the light, studies the measure, her eyes
narrowed, the very meaning of lost
woman and child.

In her body is the memory of my mouth
latched to her nipple, she and I womb to womb.
The mauve mound of my gums, silken crimson dome
of the soft palate, my heat, all a vaulted room

that awakened her first bleed of milk, the sap of her
a lake out of which she rises, welcomed
into the heartbeat stroke of the world.

My tongue's code unlocked my rune – my soul announced
to her soul in how I sucked – a kiss between strangers.
Somewhere between draw and swallow, or how
my fingers weaved at her breast, or what oozed
from my pores, she fathomed me as her dreamy one.

The bottle glints grey in the half-light.
She takes the teat in her mouth, lips
suctioned around it, not sucking but tonguing

a kiss feed of saliva; aboriginal
now as she rocks her open-eyed child,
soft grunts popping from her throat.

My First Sky

This love between us, Mother, I call a pup
tied to a tree.

The pup play growls at the conifer from the chain's limits,
pulls, pulls, wriggles her head, stiffens gangly legs
into balding grass;

strives to corkscrew her neck through the collar
over raw ears, then flops to the ground,
umbilical-ed.

She sings the scale of body language
on seeing you – leaps, yawns a mouth so moist.
Her tongue trembles to lick your fingers, face.

Braced against the chain, she stands upright,
pawing air – a juggler tossing desires,
suddenly supine, offering

her pink mottled belly; front legs reaching
like a child's arms from the depths of a cot;
hind legs splayed like a mollifying lover.

You were my first sky in this love between us.
The sun glowed. The moon shone. I saw
stars' ghost light, and the darkness
between them.

How It Starts

I get that nervous feeling I always have around her,
my mother upright against the pillows, birch-like,
papery pale and narrow. Always I do what she asks,

dishes washed, the corners swept – the perfection
of a child otherwise invisible, so when she called out
from her bedroom I wondered what is it now.

I've a pain in my head like the sound of a train
whistle, she says. Her eyes are too round, her forehead
too glossy, my school bus energy at odds with the room's

dank 5 o'clock odour. I know that she stunts me,
that the money I robbed from her purse this morning
is how I steal into my life.

Hold my head, she says, a child's story of playground hurt
in her voice. She hasn't spoken all day. Hard to believe
that she rocked me as I suckled,

that she spread my thighs with a washcloth slick
with soap. I do not doubt that she loves me obliquely
– like the moon mirrors the sun's light.

I cup the heat of her scalp. My palms absorb her heartbeat
through her damp, limp hair – a crowning. She gives
herself to my hands, covers them with her hands:
a changeling –

she can touch and can be touched. I'm almost terrified.
Her sea-green jugular, delicate as a circuit to the heart,
embodies the moment – the inference of exposure
to attack.

After the Doctor Tells Her

Bound to the bed rails in white straps, my mother's arms
flap like a fledgling testing its wings. *This is not a hospital.*
I'm four beds back from her loud mouth
on the late-night ward, her face spectacular
without the skirt of black hair. Eyes dark
as sinkholes in ice, she chants, *This is not a hospital.*
How fiercely she stares. It is painful
to hear her jackhammer mantra;
to see her hardworking hands cuffed.
The air clots between us – confusion rising
like cream. This is my mother, alone,
ablaze, glassy as a photo negative. She is afraid.
How close her fear always was, blunted by chore
upon chore throughout her clockwork days.
She is so deep within herself that the night is a cave
around her; darkness like the darkness
in which we forged a god from thunder.
For all our toil towards language, our jabber
of vowels and syllables, words
will not soothe her now:
the sound of sorrow only,
only the tempo of love.

My Mother Returns from Hospital

The moment
is like the moment
I watched a fledgling's
feather float
        through
the
      on
and
       off
  of
     time,
           dun
as the music of a cello.

I postpone her shaved head
until my next breath;
for now, the u-shaped scar
above her right ear
like a flog of liquorice,
its hue the silence of birds
when dark falls.

Blue-banded cups and plates
are piled in the sink. The to and fro
          of   a
                 bluebottle's
   buzz.

Her scalp is cygnet grey,
the wash of iodine
a marigold map
to the scalpel, drill, the clamp
that held her head sure.
She wanders the house

wearing her green coat
over her stained nightdress,
scapulars as necklace,

calm as a swan that coasts.

Bathing My Mother's Scar

Nurse Begley says,
Cup her chin in the palm of your left hand.
I gawk at the blue basin – vertical ribs
on its round body; the turned down rim
deep enough to grip. I should be back at school.
Late September sun rubs the tired day against the window.
I stand on a blade of light. On the table, a glass bottle of
something bubblegum-pink Nurse Begley brought
and added to the water, the space around it blasted,
as though it humbles light, like a snake. My mother
sits between us, her white nightdress and the pup seal
heads of her exposed knees under her green coat,
hands clamped between her legs like a child
– it's what she does to steady them.
I look outside at the pineapple-yellow leaves of the ash,
no other coloured leaf, as though the tree heard a song
about the end of summer. Solitude is all I want;
to sing to myself and not remember the sounds
from my mother's room at night, where I know
she sits in bed with the Sacred Heart picture,
the frame big as a window she could escape through.
How not to recall her voice, how not to imagine
the diaphragm lifting the robin wing-like lungs up
and out; the bellows of the lungs crashing
pink-lipped vocal folds together: dying sounds
like D minor, and D minor is a long night that slumps
towards dawn. Nurse Begley agitates the water. Rainbow
bubbles cling to her fingers. *Sponge the scar without chafing.*
The aura around my mother's bowed head is baptismal,
the rosary underway beneath her breath. The wound
above her right ear is puckered, like a mouth that cursed.

My Mother Speaks to Me

When she tells me, she only says,
The Royal Doulton tea set is yours.

It's as though we've just risen
from the rosary, weightless

after the murmured melody of voices.
I've bought my first pair of jeans

about which she knows nothing:
my body deafened by its script of leaving.

Final Visit to Her Homeplace

Aunt Monica asks me, *Does she always sleep this long?*
My mother's upstairs in bed, in her sister's house,
terminally ill, but I don't know that. All of us
turned up there the day before, three unkempt
children – she'd already taken leave of us,
and our father mostly circled the Morris Minor.

It was a day of going from house to house,
of tea and sandwiches in parlours
where everyone sat around
like they were at a funeral.
They spoke among themselves,
a background hum in reverence
of my mother's turbaned head. She looked
from face to face, bowed slowly, a vow
known only to her; and, as though for relief,
she'd then look at the sepia photos of elders
on the walls, their eyes fixed on her as if they'd
recognised themselves. When the talk lulled
there was the tick-tock-tick; shepherdess figurines
and Staffordshire dogs on the mantelpiece.
I wouldn't mind if I never again saw home.

The truth was there in their huddled goodbyes:
uncle clasped uncle, and everyone hugged
my grandmother, and Aunt Monica spun
like a top from one to the other; and my mother,
she was the only one not to cry.

Aunt Monica's face is wrinkled
as though someone's taken a pencil
and lined her like a winter tree, her mouth
so firmly shut that furrows on her top lip
blend with grooves on her lower one,

lips so completely sealed that I hear all
she is telling me – she’s afraid,
and I’m the one with the answers.

Her Last Day

When I search for my mother's bicycle in the shed
I find it behind a pile of hessian sacks, a wooden ladder
minus numerous rungs, and a brown armchair
from which yellow foam erupts: all this rubbish
to shift and I must go see my mother in hospital.
I brake hard rounding Power's corner, freewheel
downhill from there to Rahilly's Cross.
The day blurs bold and worn in October light.
As I push towards the humpback railway bridge
the back wheel goes flat. I'm so tired, tired
of being hungry, alone; aimless days
and sleepless nights in a drunk's house.
I kick the spokes.
The hospital's heat tramples me
as though I'm under earth's skin.
Turn left, up the stairs. Another left,
up more stairs. A nurse with a blue clipboard
tells me that visiting time is almost over, and then
I walk down the ward to my mother
in the last bed. Her body flat, asleep. I must sit,
but the family at the next bed has her chair.
She looks noble, the nasal cannula torc-like.
The unruffled covers and pillows, her arms
by her sides and the tent of her feet.
No Lucozade. No flowers. No cards.
As I've seen on *Marcus Welby, M.D.*,
I tilt over and kiss her forehead. I never kissed her
in my life, she wasn't that sort of mother.
What I recall now is not her face,
or her breath's measure, but the shadow
I cast, its form like a cloak that broadened
as I moved into a slot that held us both – her tribe
clamouring through molecules of smell from my glands,
enveloping her in love for the journey.

My Grandmother's Kitchen:
Sketch at 14

You've filled out nicely, haven't you! He reeks
of Old Spice and must be a relative – brown eyes
laden as a dam, mist-grey hair wispy
at his weathered neck. Her people
buried my mother today. The cortège purred
through the familiar Morris Minor route
from Limerick to Galway; the drystone walls
suddenly precious. It's as though we buried her
along the way.
Neighbours jostle at the table for ham sandwiches
and alcohol. My grandmother wanders from parlour
to kitchen, alone, bewildered by a wake without
a body; my mother's mother, a Russian Doll layer:
my life within a life, within another
of which I'm ignorant. Not everyone
here knows my last name; my mother
still the girl who left; the kitchen a novel
where I appear late in the story. Outside,
my father zigzags across the yard – a toy
with rundown batteries. For months,
I've wanted someone to hold me, to white lie
that everything will be ok. Old Spice moves
closer, puce veins web the tip of his nose, *I'd say
the fellahs are chasin' you*. Pleasure darkens his mouth.
I feel his loneliness, his backstreets of longing –
my first time to sense why my mother let go.

Mother Love

after Lola Ridge

Her love was moonlight
turning beautiful things to shadow.

I once told myself a different story.
Now, she is less image in my memory,
more echo.

I hear her in the whirl of dry oak leaves
on autumn nights; a sound mistaken for
the footfall of the dead across the earth on Samhain.

My Mother's Will

To the Maguires, the neighbours: my high hedge,
gleaming windows and locked gate.
To my daughter: the clock with the missing minute hand.
To my eldest son: my apron strings.
To my middle son: my maroon and white silk scarf.
To my youngest son: the 5 candles from his birthday cake.
To my husband: our daughter.
To Monica my sister: my stationery and pens,
sewing machine, knitting needles
and Royal Doulton tea set.
To my daughter in addition: my children, poultry,
geraniums and wedding ring.
To the Maguires in addition: the tablecloth
that blew from their clothesline and their children's
football.

WINDFALLS

after Li-Young Lee

I collect the last of the year's windfalls.
Half-bare branches droop under autumn
cloud; my bare head stung with droplets.
Twilight rustles; a smoke-grey owl coasts
through shadow.

As a child I watched my mother saunter
among the apple trees, talking to herself;
her homeplace accent fluttering the folds
of her mouth. She paused to listen, smile;
laughing at herself, I thought.

Nutmeg and clove, sugared apple juice
in buttery pastry; oven odours
in my nightfall kitchen; a change
in the thrusts of wind addling the window.

Is it my mother crooning amid the trees
in her orchard language? I almost call to her.
I draw back the white voile, see swaying branches
stroke each other.

How I Would Bury My Mother

after Rachel McKibbens

Close to the ocean
and sheer cliffs; close
to rock-strewn fields,
the brown hawk;
close to the edge
of this valley;
I would release her
from this soundless
graveyard.

For all the hope
she lost; for every
name and hurt
that found her;
I will set her
in the blood
of my womb;
will carry her,
cherish her
as the only child
I will ever know.

Life Lesson

I never saw it coming. There was nothing
in how I knew Aunt Monica that prepared me;
my mother's sister, the first adult to address me
as an adult: I am 4, exploring the novelty of her
staircase. She sits with me on the fourth step,
shares the sad fact that this is as far as I can go,
Until you're 5. Count to 5 for me.

Their letters were regular; Aunt Monica's
homeplace gossip in biro, pencil, or both;
always on pages torn from a copybook.
I recall her Christmas parcel; a goose on the train
from Galway, wrapped in layers of cardboard;
unplucked, its headless neck bound in bloody
newspaper, yielding her home's odour –
turf smoke's memory of bog cotton.

I stayed a week with her after my mother's funeral.
It was still ceremony; hours and days astray
in white mugs of sweet tea. Aunt Monica
roamed the rooms, kneaded her hands; broke
out in, *Hail Holy Queen, Mother of mercy.*
I thought it was more prayer when she said,
Can I have her coat?

SOOTHSAYER

Even now I wonder at how calm I remain
face to face with my father
on the 8 o'clock doorstep.
He says, *Your mother's dead.*
He says, *Phone Galway.*
His mouth a spew of umber and amber vowels
moulds the autumn morning
into a pane of glass suddenly holed
at its centre. Fine lines rift outward
until the lot shatters shard by rainbow
-flecked shard at our feet; jumbled
jigsaw, each piece whole as a life.

Onto the morning air I hang the cut
of glass with his name:

Grey Tam; rim dry-sweat-stiff as a horse collar,
wrung like a rag in bony, hard-knuckled hands
when talking to his betters,
fucking them off afterwards.

Over and over I turn the glass fragment he tosses
to me; feel him cream-lick my slow knowing
that my reflex of catching the glass spike
makes me just another peeler of spuds,
washer of pots and pans.
I slot my piece next to his; wedges simulating the sad
sorry trinity: Father, daughter, the holy mother.

Her name: Busy Hands: fingers stubby as a servant's,
gnarled from needing no one; neighbours wondering
at themselves in her kitchen the day of the ambulance.

I thumb the last segment in place; mosaic
of pale bone and blue vein dazzle
complex as an iris, or a heart;
click of the gate as it closes behind my father,
and I crystal clear in knowing
the wrong one has died.

About the Author

Breda Spaight lives in County Limerick. Her work has appeared in *Poetry Ireland Review, Southword, Cyphers, Ambit, Crannóg, Banshee* and 'New Irish Writing', *Irish Independent*. She was featured poet in *The Stinging Fly* and *The Interpreter's House*, and was among the poets in the *Best New British and Irish Poets 2018* anthology from Eyewear. She was chosen for the Poetry Ireland introductions series, and the introductions reading at the Cork International Poetry Festival. She has won the Doolin Poetry Prize, the Boyle Arts Festival Poetry Prize, and was shortlisted for the Cúirt New Writing Prize, iYeats International Poetry Prize, and the Red Line Poetry Prize. She was a finalist twice in the Aesthetica Creative Writing Award. Her debut chapbook, *The Untimely Death of My Mother's Hens*, was published by Southword Editions in the New Irish Voices series. She holds an M.Phil. in creative writing from Trinity College, Dublin. *Watching for the Hawk* is her debut collection.